Tim
BERNERS~LEE

Damian Harvey

Illustrated by Judy Brown

W
FRANKLIN WATTS
LONDON•SYDNEY

Contents

CHAPTER 1
Trainspotting

When Timothy Berners-Lee was born in 1955, the world was very different to the one that you and I know today. People didn't have computers or games consoles in their homes, and TV programmes were in black and white, with just one channel!

Tim grew up in South West London. At school, Tim wasn't very good at sports,

but he loved maths and science.

His school had two busy train lines running past either side of it. Tim was fascinated by all the trains that he saw passing by and he started to make a note of the different ones that he spotted.

Like lots of other boys, Tim had a model railway in his bedroom. He loved watching the model trains racing around the tracks, disappearing into the tunnels, then returning to the station.

To make his design even better, Tim
made gadgets to control the trains.
He soon became more interested in
electronics than in trains.

Tim's mum, Mary Lee Woods, and his dad, Conway Berners-Lee, were mathematicians and computer programmers. Together, they had worked on some of the world's first computers.

They were sure that, one day, computers could be programmed to do anything. They loved sharing their exciting ideas with their son.

One day, Tim came home from school to find his father reading a book about the human brain.

His father was wondering how the brain connected odd things together...like smelling something that instantly makes you think of another place that you've been to.

While his father wondered if computers could connect things in the same way, Tim went off to do his homework. But those little thoughts stayed in his mind.

CHAPTER 2
Tv to Computer

After leaving school, Tim went to Oxford University. Although he loved maths, he decided to study physics – the science that looks at natural matter and energy.

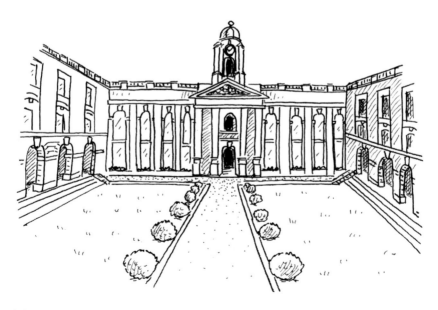

He thought this would be more useful because he would learn about light, sound, heat, electronics, mechanics and the structure of atoms that make up everything in the universe.

As an experiment, Tim bought an old television set from a repair shop and used it to build himself a computer.

In 1976, Tim graduated from Oxford University with a first class degree in physics. He couldn't wait to start programming computers and building things for himself.

At first he worked for a couple of different companies on things like barcode technology and then writing special software for printers.

Then, in 1980, Tim went to do some work for CERN, the European Organisation for Nuclear Research, in Geneva, Switzerland.

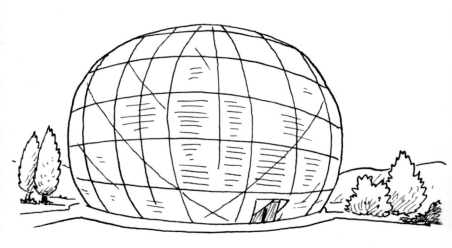

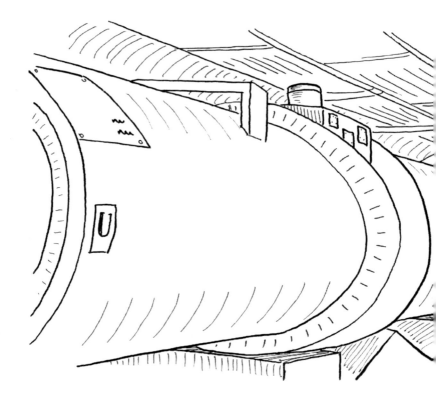

Lots of scientists and university professors from all over the world work at CERN. They use huge machines to help them discover new things about the smallest particles in the universe.

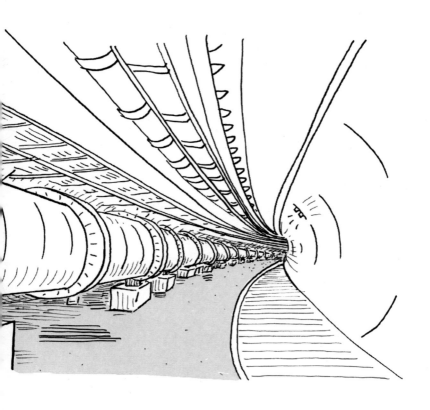

Tim went there to work on
computer software that could
help scientists store and look
at information collected from
their experiments.

While working at CERN, Tim grew tired of spending so much time trying to find information that was stored on many different people's computers.

Because the people at CERN came from so many different places, it meant that their computers were different too. Tim had to learn how to use them all.

CHAPTER 3
Sharing Ideas

To make his work easier, Tim wrote some computer programs that helped him take information from one computer and put it onto another one.

This was a great step forward but Tim was sure there must be a better way of doing it.

He wondered if all the computers could be linked together so that information could be shared quickly and easily. Then he remembered an old book he had seen on his parent's bookshelf.

Enquire
Within
upon
Everything

The book was called
Enquire Within Upon Everything.

It had first been written in 1856
when Queen Victoria was on the
throne but Tim had been fascinated
by it. Just imagine how wonderful it
would be to have a book that told
you everything you wanted to know
about anything.

The book was full of hints and advice. It told you what to do if you wanted to bake bread, choose a wife or bury a relative. In fact, *Enquire Within Upon Everything* was the perfect place to look for anything that you wanted to know.

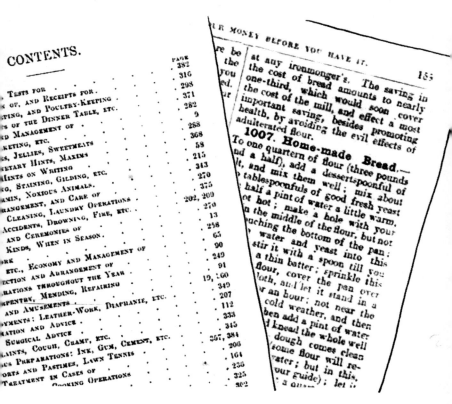

CONTENTS.

R MONEY BEFORE YOU HAVE IT.

185

re be at any ironmonger's. The saving in the cost of bread amounts to nearly one-third, which would soon cover the cost of the mill, and effect a most important saving, besides promoting health, by avoiding the evil effects of adulterated flour.

1007. Home-made Bread.— To one quartern of flour (three pounds and a half), add a dessertspoonful of salt, and mix them well: mix about two tablespoonfuls of good fresh yeast in half a pint of water a little warm, but not hot: make a hole with your fist in the middle of the flour, but not touching the bottom of the pan: pour water and yeast into this, stir it with a spoon till you make a thin batter; sprinkle this over with flour, cover the pan over with a cloth, and let it stand in a warm place for an hour: not near the fire in cold weather, and then add a pint of water: knead the whole well till the dough comes clean (some flour will require more water; but in this, your experience must be your guide): let it ...

23

To help him find all the
information on the different
computers at CERN, Tim wrote
a 'web-like' program.

He named it 'ENQUIRE' after
the old book. Working with the
'ENQUIRE' program gave Tim
the idea of creating something that
could keep on growing in a way
that the old book could not.

The space in books is limited by the number of pages and Tim wanted to create a space big enough to hold all of the ideas and thoughts that everyone might have.

He knew computers could not give us all the information that we wanted, but they could help by making the information easier to find. Instead of having to read hundreds of books, computers could do it for us. They could even give us the information at the press of a button.

Tim thought it would be even better if people could keep adding to the information so that it was always new and up to date. This would mean that the 'shared knowledge' would grow and spread even faster than it could in a printed book.

CHAPTER 4
World Wide Web

Tim knew that what he had to do was build a framework that would connect all the world's computers together. It might sound like a small step now, but it was a giant leap that would completely change people's lives all over the world.

He decided to call his framework the World Wide Web.

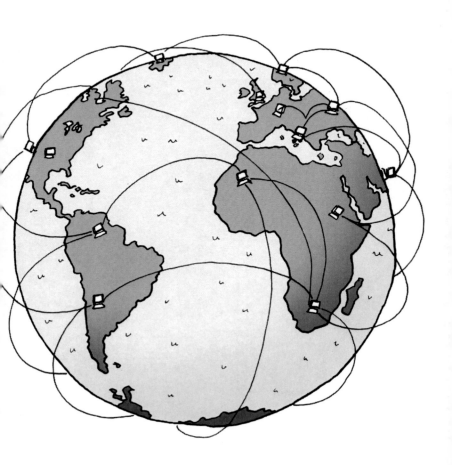

Luckily, Tim didn't have to do all of the work as there were other people around the world working on computer technology too. Some people had created ways of giving computers their own names and addresses.

Some had developed 'email' and others had created 'hyperlinks' so you could open a document by clicking on a link (but they couldn't open documents on other computers around the world).

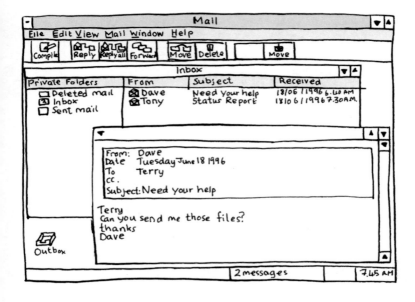

On 11th March 1989, Tim submitted
his idea for the World Wide Web
to Mike Sendall, his boss at CERN.
Mike thought the idea was 'exciting'
but nothing happened.

Tim didn't give up. He and his friend Robert Cailliau started working together whilst doing other jobs. Robert was good at getting other people to take notice of Tim's fantastic idea. Eventually, Tim's boss bought him the very latest 'NeXT' computer so he could work on his idea.

Tim developed the world's first web browser and created the world's first website using the 'NeXT' computer. In 1991, he launched the world's very first website –
http://info.cern.ch

The website might look very boring because it didn't have pictures, sound or moving graphics but it told people all about the World Wide Web (WWW). It was a giant stepping stone towards reaching the internet that we have today.

Coming up with the idea of the
WWW was easy for Tim. The hard
part would be getting the rest of
the world to make their computers
communicate using the same
language.

He knew that people always liked to
do things their own way but he also
knew that the WWW wouldn't work
if everyone did things differently.
So in April 1993, CERN made
the WWW software available for
everyone to use – free of charge.

People quickly realised that Tim's idea was brilliant. They started building computers that could all talk to each other in the same language, HTML (Hyper Text Markup Language) that web browsers in computers can read.

```html
<!DOCTYPE html>
<html id="home-layout">
  <head>
    <meta http-equiv="content-type"
    <title>Source Code Pro</title>
      <!-- made with <3 and AFDKO -->
    <meta name="keywords" content="sans,
      monospace, open source, coding,
    <link rel="stylesheet" type="text/css
  </head>
  <body>
```

Tim was amazed to see how quickly his idea was spreading around the world, and today it's hard to imagine a world without it.

CHAPTER 5
Awards and Prizes

In 1995, Tim and Robert Cailliau were given an award for their work on the World Wide Web by the Association of Computing Machinery. It was to be the first of many...

In 1997, Tim received an OBE (Order of the British Empire) for services to global computer networking. In 2004, he was knighted by Queen Elizabeth II and in 2007 the Queen awarded him the Order of Merit (OM).

Then, in 2013, she awarded Tim and four other computer engineers 'The Queen Elizabeth Prize for Engineering'.

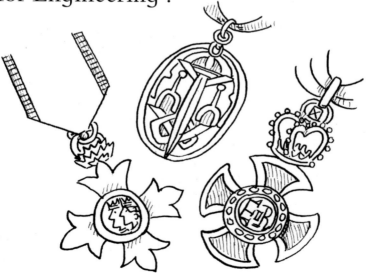

Since creating the WWW, Tim hasn't stopped working. Today he still works with other people to make his dream of the World Wide Web grow and become even better. It's an amazing way of sharing information and ideas.

Tim has always worked to make sure the WWW belongs to everyone so they can share their thoughts, their ideas and their dreams.

In 2009, the British Prime Minister, Gordon Brown, asked Tim to help the British Government by making information on their computers easier to access by the people.

Tim Berners-Lee's dream was to create a place where people could share information freely. He never dreamed of fame and fortune and he likes to keep his private life to himself – but in 2012 many people around the world saw him for the first time.

At the opening ceremony of the 2012 Summer Olympic Games in London, Tim sat at a desk in the very centre of the stadium and sent his message to the world…

"THIS IS FOR EVERYONE!"

Timeline

1955   June 8th: Timothy Berners-Lee is born in South West London.

1976   He graduates from Queen's College, Oxford University with a degree in physics.

1980   Tim produces the first 'Hypertext' system 'ENQUIRE' for his own use whilst doing consultancy work at CERN.

1989   11th March - submitts his idea for WWW - The World Wide Web.

1990   Tim develops a prototype WWW on the NeXT computer with the first web browser.

1991   First website launches, http://info.cern.ch which gives people information about WWW.

1993   30th April: CERN puts WWW software into the public domain.

1994   World Wide Web Consortium is founded.

1995	Tim and Robert Cailliau are given ACM (Association of Computer Machinery) System Software award.
1997	Tim is awarded the OBE for services to global computer networking.
2004	Tim is knighted by Queen Elizabeth II.
2007	Tim is awarded the Order of Merit (OM) by Queen Elizabeth II.
2009	Prime Minister Gordon Brown enlists Tim's help in making government information more accessible to the public.
2012	Tim takes part in the opening ceremony for the Olympic Games in London. His message – 'This Is For Everyone' – is tweeted around the world and appears in huge letters around the stadium.
2013	Queen Elizabeth II awards Tim and four other computer engineers 'The Queen Elizabeth Prize for Engineering'. Their award is for work since the 1970s which led to the development of the internet and the WWW.

First published in 2014 by
Franklin Watts
338 Euston Road
London NW1 3BH

Franklin Watts Australia
Level 17/207 Kent Street
Sydney NSW 2000

HB ISBN 978 1 4451 3320 1
PB ISBN 978 1 4451 3322 5
Library ebook ISBN 978 1 4451 3323 2
ebook ISBN 978 1 4451 3324 9

Dewey Decimal Classification Number: 004'.092

Series editor: Melanie Palmer
Series designer Cathryn Gilbert

Printed in Great Britain

Franklin Watts is a division of Hachette Children's Books,
an Hachette UK company.
www.hachette.co.uk